AF593432

Grand Opening

I took a ride in the ancient alleys

To the narrow streets of big cities

Under the shade of the beaming sun stream

With the wavering tress of high hills

Gliding through the drowsy miles

Fusing with the belt of new time.

A lone walk in a dark silent hall,

Numb tongue with a faint heart,

Losing her pictures from my wall,

Big cheers, watch the curtains fall.

Zoning out in the tracks of rock,

Futile graves of broken hearts.

Catastrophic evaluation, mindful evaporation,

In the heat of one last hour,

Midst the squeeze of the clock.

Hibernating life waking up to the other side,

Cold clumsiness doesn't hide,

Sudden prowl of prey, dusty winds have gone astray.

Cold vigorous clouds,

Spiraling in the thunderstorms,

Brave graves of stolen hearts.

Walking a lonely mile,

Every time there's a heartbreak,

A dam breaks in her eyes,

How can I find a break?

A break from all that's broken apart,

Broken from all that's built to fall apart,

I've been a dog hanging on your leash,

Switching lanes just to find some peace,

Where this heart faints to sing,

Slowly unfolding a story,

All and forever, stars shine fall like a feather,

Rivers sever and flow on forever,

At least in my dreams,

At least in my dreams.

You and me,

Were made to be,

In a love story.

You and I,

Will live a life,

Of eternity,

Making love in the paradise.

Curtains of clouds, fall and rise

Searching here and anywhere,

For that little sunshine,

I'm just a man on a velvet flight,

Bound to fall for a thousand times,

Willing to stand for a thousand and one.

You and me in this life

Are all synchronized,

Just like the planets

Around the sun.

It’s all one and mystified.
What you hide inside
Is my secret I confide.

The night is just dark,

Until you go one step further.

You are nothing but blind,

Until you go one step further.

Until you go one step further,

For the answer you long,

Like the child for his mother,

For the freedom you lost,

Like a child to his mother.

Your home is a pile of bricks,

Until you go one step further.

All your dreams are unborn,

Until you go one step further.

Until you go one step further,

For the answer you long,

Like the child for his mother,

For the freedom you lost,

Like a child to his mother.

If only you could feel,

The dance of the wind,

Can give you chills,

Shape all your ways.

They could never make,

Steer you to a place,

They could never take.

Everything you ever wished for,

Stands abandoned,

On the other side of the bridge,

On the other side of the bridge.

Ride along the edge,

It's time to claim your life,

Watch the past sink in the time.

Ride along the edge,

To the other side of the bridge.

So now we know the sun goes down,
When at night the stars come out.
So now we know the lights drifts down,
From the fear of a circus clown.

Better break these chains of train,
Or else that's where you will remain.
There's no shame to walk naked,
As the rain washes away your stains.

You know your world got turned and twirled,
The sun and the stars are all from the afterworld.
The moon can still bloom a caged heart,
My loved one, the wind is crying for you, don't stop.

I feel like letting go,

When there is nothing to hold

Our blood is stained by the wretched bleeding heart.

Which dreams a lot from a clear start

But the stairway is nowhere near.

I wish I had something more to say,

But the colors are turning grey.

But I'll find my way and walk away,

Through the raining storm,

Through the sunshine.

Whatever comes my way to get there,

I'll take another ride,

Until the last star dies,

Until the last star dies,

Until the last star dies.

When it gets dark,

When it gets too dark to step outside.

Poor and unwary blood rises with the tide.

When killers parade on with pride,

Rich men tie their golden ties,

And their wives live a diamond life.

It's time to leave our olden ways behind,

To see the Sun colour the whole sky,

To face the truth; that is so wrong,

For a new spring in the dark paradise.

Learn to see it through,

A newborn with a silver spoon,

In this dangerous town after the sundown,

When the shadows come out to play

And kill the day,

All the children hide and pray,

Waiting for the sun to shine again.

Something in the wind wipes them away,

Like the darkest clouds falling down to rain,

And the sky blows up in flames,

For a new ray in the paradise.

For a new day in the paradise

When you are on your own,

And there's no light in your home,

Your eyes will spark the candles,

And bloom the colour back into new.

The world will remember you

Until the last star dies,

Until the last star dies.

When you are on your own,

Engulfed with the silence all alone,

Wicked voices tend to get close,

Is your heart scared to know more?

Waves will take you to the shore,

Until the last star dies,

Until the last star dies.

There is someone keeping an eye on me,

Whenever I try to speak,

It holds my tongue on a razor blade.

I try to think, then I strum my strings,

Was I too naive to believe in me

And not someone else?

But the Man in the Mirror tells no one,

Tells no one,

Tells no one.

I try to think, but the thought stinks,

The thought of wearing that filthy shoe that doesn't fit

And doesn't suit me a bit;

Kills me, but it thrills me.

So I hurl it out of my mind and shredded it into bits

Wind my keys, the ballerina speaks,

She swirls and she twirls and she whirls,

Wearing her pearls.

She unfurls like a flower and she is my girl

Wonder how it feels to be lost in a music box.

Who is there? Shrouding like a shadow,

Trying to fill a hollow time with sorrow.

With some joy left in me, come ride with me.

If you can keep up, run with me, jump with me,

Sing with me, and dance with me.

Where is your spirit that was guiding you home,

Gone by the longing that is lost in your bones.

Where is your spirit to be you

And not what you were told?

Gone by the longing that was lost in your bones.

Do you know who you are?

And how it feels to get lost in the stars

Come here, let’s disappear into the sea.

Come and get raped by the breeze

Come and let me take you to the streets,

Where the lost souls dream.

I was burning like a candle,

Then you came at me like a gale,

Since that day,

I've been treading against these hails.

For how long can I deny,

Deny the falling rain.

Can you really tell, who rings the bell.

No, you haven't got the answer,

Just like everyone else.

An empty seashell

An empty seashell

Are the bruises erased,

After I embellished you with wreath?

How was it so easy for you to believe?

Believe in all that wasn't me.

But the door was always open,

And will always be,

why don't you just leave?

It was never enough, it will never be,

I'm not satisfied and why should I be.

This man inside hides like a gentle breeze,

So when you breathe,

it fills your life with all his melodies.

But when you leave,

It brings dark clouds to share his grief.

And the rain falls like love,

That was never meant to be.

Can you get a grip of the answer

Before it evanesces in the breeze?

Hold up, breathe in, and don't freeze.

You are under control, digging a hole under a tree.

Cut those roots that hold you and bind you,

And make you crawl beneath the ease.

You are not their marionette anymore,

Don't look down and take control

And hear the king roar.

In my head, I sit alone

Trying to close the door,

But some whisper comes,

Whistling through my core.

I run to the store,

To find my folks,

They sit there straddling,

All across the seashore.

Hearing the waves crash,

With our marooned coast,

You want to hear me out,

But I'm lost for words

We are lost for words

Now that you've come home,

Dragged your feet along the shore,

I want to know,

How far did you see,

And how far did you go?

When you closed your eyes,

The stars; they hide in hive.

When you rise and shine,

I kissed you for the first time,

And I wonder, was I yours and were you mine,

Then for the first time, I kissed you goodbye.

That noose you draw,

Is not in my hands to untie.

Those flowers that blossom,

Are all grey without you, sunshine.

Rain that slides down the roof,

Opening doors of spring,

Comes flooded back with memories.

Dust that blocks my sight,

Settles down as time passes by,

Hisses in my ear,

Like a snake, tangling my fear.

Kisses me and slithers away,

Into the evanesce of night.

Late tales of the dead and lost,

Strange times reaching to colossal heights,

a clutter of dimes and echoes of rhymes.

Torn pockets, a man held at gunpoint,

Bribed women sticking heads to their groin.

Hinges and latches broken down,

Traces of an intruder,

Bathtub overflowing with joy.

An empty house with lights out,

a convict doing some inside job.

Precious metals stolen,

Someone deems there was a person

in eldritch garb, dancing late at night.

A ghost or a shadow,

Which is more real in this eerie life?

Trails of frail steps,

she snaps and backs out saying

“something isn't right tonight.

I need to see someone but

I'm going out with someone else tonight,
It's been frittering away my precious time."
She sardonically jitters while playing with her hair,
"Death is an old friend of mine,
Come sit with me with no fear and live your life."

Hand me the keys, come with me,
Let's go to the wild side.
Yes! We are almost there,
Roll down your window and let the wind, sing and jive.
Camphor Moon holds a frame in her jaded eyes.

Love is a bullet for a heart,

which no vest can guard,

Be the first one to take the shot,

So open fire, there's no reason to stop.

Gunpowder; where will we ponder?

When thoughts turn darker

And sounds become louder,

Your feet dabble faster,

And everything becomes palaver.

But a heart that's fuelled has been screwed,

Still beats when the bullet skids through,

Nothing can end this spirit that's in you,

Yes, we are through

And I'm never getting back to you.

In the night,

I stayed awake with a little hope and a tiny tear.

Needles ran to elope round and round,

Slamming all the doors, bashing glass to the floor.

The cold gale blew in through my window,

Snuffed out my last drop of fire,

Before I could kindle the pyre.

Darkness spattered my attic,

A ghost soughed with frantic haste,

And toppled my ancient urn.

Tramping through the windswept streams,

How erotically moonlight filled the breeze,

Something I could have never dreamed.

There are lies hiding underneath that tree,

I walked as blinded as I could be,

But these eyes steered me to see,

Lifted my deception

And gave me a shadow to walk along with me.

I'm longing for a ride,

I'm burning this night to ashes tonight,

I'm tearing this whole sky to the ground tonight,

I'm going out for a ride,

I'm wearing no mask tonight,

I'll purge through this unkind wind tonight.

In the morning,

Sunlight came blooming, everybody kept yawning.

Dreamers doused in heat and kept drowning.

Wisemen left us behind to be alive and crowning.

Jesters came playing the bagpipes

Leaving behind the worn-out fights

Cruise on and on, crash into the tides.

Keep on cruising higher,

Taste the flavour of seven seas

efore they dry,

And let the storm be in your eyes,

If you fall deep stay there

Till the very end.

No need to crush your mind

Let your paper boat sail away,

Don’t believe you'll see it ever again.

Look through the meadows of the horizon,

Explore miles of uncertain expression,

Singing the secret quotations,

Dreaming of all the wonders.

Don't stop when the killer rows the boat,

Don't stop when the fear rocks the boat,

Don't be afraid,

When the snake slithers out of the burrow.

Be wildered and wild.

Serve to strive and stride to survive,

Let your tongue taste the bewildered spice.

Bury your bloated shadow into the sands of time,

Empty your chambers, it’s time to rise.

Grand gestures of molten rhyme,

Glide on the gemmed lake,

Till the very end of the time

Rolling with the stone

Feelings get lost in the bones

Hiding under the feathers of chrome

Gliding through the winter afterglow

Strolling under the falling sky

Where the birds learn to fly

There we roam, there we roll

Until the end of the time

A titled boat, shunned beside the river,

Gentle water drifts past by like a mirror,

Only lonely hand feeling a shiver,

Heavy clouds fall apart the quickest,

Filling the levee to the fullest,

As the rings of the chain began to take turns,

Something drowned forever, so we learned.

A still boat,

Shunned beside the labyrinth

of a river like a dusty mirror,

Only lonely hands,

Holding a strong grip of a cold shiver,

Heavy clouds fall apart the quickest,

Filling the levee to the fullest,

As the rings of the chain began to take turns,

Something had to sink, and we had to learn,

Meet me at the next turn,

Meet me at the next turn.

Lost somewhere between the lines,

Keen to know what's on your mind,

Feeding on heat

Because the Sun is there to remind,

Rewind the twisted mind

And glide on the wind when

it's inclined.

A broken mirror still reflecting what's mine,

Turning the page, reading between the lines,

Obscured by the wall

And a woman spilling piles of lies,

Stretched my thoughts above and beyond,

Now the truth is in her eyes

Crown head breaking the neck,

Grips on a cold steel wreak,

Spent time in the deep well,

Knocked down the door to hell,

Only one now, that should ring a bell.

Let your wings unfurl and learn to fly,

Just to forget,

Moving forward to leave it all behind.

Brain dead from great depth

World wrecked and world rampaged

I'm out and about, grab yourself

Let's travel galaxies, let's build new fallacies

Pick it up from where the world left

Come and stay, to the next break of day,

Forgetting to pull the brakes,

Let's drive in daze, straight into the maze,

A steady gaze for a new craze.

Newborn eyes opening to a latent dream,

We shall walk straight through

this labyrinth of a stream.

Wonder if it’s a fallacy, love feels alchemy,

my heart’s only remedy

Don’t tease me, it tells you helplessly

I do what I love and love what I do to you.

In my dream, my awakening dream.

Was it love or just a flying machine,

Took me high and washed me clean,

Just like the waves coming out of the sea,

Let me love you, and glide on the breeze,

It's so easy if you want it to be.

I want to paint the sky for you,

I want to spin this world for you,

Hold my heart and let's fly to the moon,

Love me under the falling sky,

Love me under the star-light,

Sit by my side, be here with me tonight,

Before it's time for goodbye.

Wish you were mine

Wish you were mine

Wish you were mine

Have you ever seen the rain,

coming down on a sunny day

When a storm is just a mile away

We are going on an uncertain holiday

Remember how Mama used to tell you?

Let the sky- blue fly over you,

Let the clouds glide over you,

Let the river flow down to you,

Let those fears subside like rain down the drain.

And then when we shine, it's the new light we gain,

We start again when nothing remains,

We burn so fast in the dark train,

When the brightest candle goes out in the rain.

You used to be so amused,

What made you so confused?

You look frozen, let's break the ice,

No more crawling, it's time to rise.

Let me gaze into your eyes,

What's the price of these lies?

If anyone of us dies,

Will the other one stand by and say goodbye?

Cause' we promised to go on till the end,

And never leave each other's side,

And never let our love die,

And if that's a lie,

I don't even want to try,

And if that's a lie,

I just want to lie alone and cry,

And die alone and wave goodbye.

But what can I do,

When you say, "love,"

You don't know how much I love you,

I just trust you and say yes, you are mine,
Never want to break your heart,
Never want to fall apart,
Cause' I can't see a tear in your eyes,
So let me caress your thighs,
Let's do our little crime,
No need to check the time,
Cause' you are mine,
And always on my mind,
I can never leave you behind.

We are tangled in a web,
Which we just can't unwind,
So much in love still not blind;
If we never lost, how can we can ever find?

Use me, abuse me, but you can never refuse me.

Hit me, spit me, but you can never trick me.

Break me, quake me, but you can never shake me.

Shape me, rape me, but you can never escape me.

Bruise me, confuse me, so you'll never choose me.

Here I take a pledge

I'll take you to the edge,

Put you through the hedge,

Push you down the sledge

Wonder if the sky gets washed away,

Thunder comes down, flashing like a ray,

On the ground that mends your way,

You try to scream,

But your voice gets washed away

Wonder if all the stars get washed away,

Will it be the last day to shed a tear,

How will the darkness obey you, my dear.

Wonder if my dreams get washed away,

What will I have to say?

For what will my heart stray?

Wonder if the sky gets washed away,

Wonder if all the stars get washed away

Wonder if my dreams get washed away,

Wonder if these things are far away,

Wander away, wander away, wander away,

Wander away, wander away, wander away.

A drop of tear in the ocean,

An unrequited emotion,

It's a story of a girl,

Hiding underwater like a pearl.

She whirls and twirls and swirls, wearing her pearls

In her little room, she talks to the moon,

She owns a diary and writes to the gloom,

One she can't hold, one she can't mould,

In her window, like a wallpaper, it's stored.

It's you and me in this dark globe,

I'll steal your stare and bring you here,

So near that I can feel your glare,

In my eyes, I always care,

For that one thing that I bear,

A drop of tear in the ocean,

Ripples to the shore,

And brings along so much more.

Now I just stand and stare,

Through my window for just one last glare,

To look for the light that comes at night,

There is my love sleeping on the clouds,

Waiting for the moonlight,

Waiting for the moonlight.

I'm feeling this place like a ransacked nest,

Feathers falling from a beak of a guest.

Feeling this space like a growing mold,

Bloody hands digging,

a shovel to a foreign crawl,

The spattering of F-bombs;

this girl activated my doom dogs

Scribbling the blanks with jilted crayons,

Letting bygones be bygones,

colouring my book of rhymes

with tears of onions.

Washing this dirt away, I run with untied lace,

And still don't drop my face,

Riff knuckles, nothing else matters to date,

Corpse of words on a sleek blade,

Titled and wicked street lanes.

Coming to an end with wonders at night,

Thunders that fight with winds that fly,

The smell of rejoice with the sweet taste of price,

Land of sprouts cracked in drought,

Giving it a good squeeze till it drips out

Wish for the words to come out

Wish for the wor.

In this poetic harvest, I'm the reaper you forsake,

My heart is seething and my mind is grieving,

I've lost the art that I was dreaming.

Girl, you have to light the spark that's in the dark,

Face the fall and take the toll,

Get yourself back on your toes,

Feel the heat that sweats sweet and sour,

Grasp the shock of a thunderbolt,

Spill the poison from the silver spoon,

Gaze with me into the darkroom,

Spatter the ink to the jewelled moon.

I'm coming at you like a breaking news,

Because confusion hides the truth,

About the prince of the shimmering blues,

Heading for clues into the hazy view,

He found a girl and in her his hues

He found a girl and she was his muse

Nirvana from the orbiting truth,

The end of our lingering boots,

Tree of wisdom that we uproot,

Living life just to get through,

Done and dusted, desires blew,

I'm coming with a chainsaw to cut this sword
like a birthday cake,
I'm filling this page with all my thoughts that
are trapped in a cage,
Breaking through the spiral with rage.
Voices coming out of scabbard hidden in a
cupboard (piece of cake).

Now the world is on pyre and the flames
go higher, I'm losing fingers for a better tomorrow,
drawing figures of a busted cargo.
It's going back but yesterday has left no track,
They fill their tanks with your tears and leak the tap.
They use your blood to feel their nerves
and give you sweat to grab.

I'm a broken cup, you can never fill me up.
You lose your mind and they win a price,
You keep their lies intact,
Fill your wallets with black dice,
Give the mice their cheese and it runs

Without getting seized.

Don’t tell me you didn’t watch Tom and Jerry.

It’s a lost world, where to find a better word.

I know heroes don't die until the war is done,

It's forever only after the end has come.

You watched the red hot sun burn,

Now the winter has come,

We step into the day of Armageddon,

Now the whole world has succumbed.

Now I'm calling you to hear this tale,

Like a monkey trying to bite its tail,

You fritter away these days in a daze,

When the first drop of rain fell from the sky,

And the first beam of the Sun fell upon the eyes,

That was the time when the carnival began to rise,

Big wheel spins and comes around,

Giving you the ride of your life,

Changes come in their own style,

I want to smile, it's been a while.

When the massacre of innocence shrinks

the lights of heaven,

And the clock strikes eleven and you

begin to imagine,

Let it happen, don't let it blacken,

Where will it lead us in Eden?

Reach out for the light from within and

torch the beacon,

These stars don't lie,

And now my eyes can rely on the sky.

We only shine when there's no light,

We only rise when we fall from a height,

We only hide when we are afraid to ride,

We had our time and we crossed our line,

We made our move and we touched the moon,

You are on your knees, you will learn soon,

Learn to live it until it blooms.

Just like God's philosophy,

Was it love or just a fantasy?

It burns in here with great intensity,
Ones that you loved; hurt you the most.
Some call this insanity, some just inanity,
But the show must go on, moving on, its reality.

Brittle trust that held you strong, tore apart,
Your only love left you to rot,
Now you're all alone with your thoughts,
In a room tied with slip knots,
Snuffed-out candles and burn marks,
Trying to solve this enigma,
One that is called life,
One that lies behind the veil of lies,
Trying to remember, when it's time to die,
You shall comply.

How were you supposed to know?
You were just too young,
Too young to make a run,
Stunned by a gun, you are not the only one,

Now you're chasing the setting sun,

Hope you live each day like it's the last one,

Waiting for the better days to come.

Waiting for the better days to come.

Blacked out in the dark

Scratching some old scars

Melt down those chains

That hangs so tall

Keep you close to my heart

Like a girl does to her barbie doll

She cries no more but tears they fall,

Just erase that past, the future calls,

It's so unreal that I can't believe,

I'm so lost in the beauty for real.

I don't have the right words now,

When I'll find them, I'll use my mouth,

To tell you about my love for the blond,

Tell you about the girl in the red cloth,

Tell you about my perfect goth.

Come closer, kiss me till I fall,

Kiss my flame like a moth,

Climb on me and take a fall.

Don't resent me, you can have it all.

I am not what I was told to be,

I'm free but you choose not to be.

I'm falling for her but care no more,

Writing her name in the clouds above,

will it rain no more.

***Castles of clouds that washed down*,**

Reaching out tides in eclipse, lights go down.

I'm watching it all happen like

glints in a house of mirrors.

Shot her down in the suspense of a thriller.

It's a complete eclipse, a starless night.

I'm sitting in a movie theatre.

Faces come out of the shadows,
Wild horses stampeding the meadows.
A hollow fire grows narrow,
Time reminds us to dig a deeper burrow.
Find firm grip on the ground
and shoot your arrow.

Hungry bellies of gallows feast on
faceless marionettes,
Their needs increased.
Through the iron tunnel, light blinds,
Flashing at the end, secrets unwind.
Summoning broken arrows
from wars of old gods,
Rain down on dirty dirt, stories untold.
Whispering spring, a siren's call,
Brings you down,
And drowns you in its thrall.

People keep coming and going,

Kicking dust and breaking bones,

Fancy feast and ring tones,

Still, these streets live on forever.

Listening to the caller's tune

Remember the last time,

Something made you feel relentless,

Come on, jump and jive and dive,

Your red-hot blood wants to play.

Come on, run and hide and stay,

Don't give up without a fight today,

For how far we have come,

Keep dangling on the thin strings,

Beating drums and strum.

Let the music play in the Milky Way,

You carry on, I know you won't stay.

Kaleidoscopic eye gazing in the dream bowl,

Living in the darkroom;

With her pictures and perfume.

Not for anyone else but for yourself,

Watch the dead stare of truth,

For how much I've loved you,

How much you've loved me

If you could just let me live,

I'd die for you.

No one can love you like I could do,

I'd never let anything hurt you.

But our love is a troublemaker,

Cause' we are the wild kind,

Living in the jungle at the wrong time.

Your head bursts with an optic vision,

Soon your nerves begin to breakdown.

So kiss the broken girl of the downtown,

Pump fist to fist and go on dancing around

.

What's your business with the crown,

But I hope you are down to be exposed

Butt naked in the crowd,

Come dance with death in a shroud.

These pages are falling from the

weight of my thoughts,

Those dark clouds are turning

into tiny raindrops.

A fire that can't be snoozed by

the whirling wind,

Still cold enough to make you,

Forget about it,

Forget about it, forget about it.

Now I lay and watch the moon dance,

The swarm of moths burning

in a muse of trance.

I like to be in my deep trench,

With my love that lets me be.

With the one that loves to be,

With the one that sets me free.

You are the one for me.

You are a lost girl,

Singing for a lost cause,

Staring at the red Sun,

Reminiscing what night has done.

Standing in line for the rest of your life,

You make a move and some

strange eyes fall on you.

This thought once dawned on me,

Taking me back to the point,

where I broke down.

How come I've let this happen?

How come time had stretched to this point?

Now I'm crawling to the pieces that fell down,

Here is a kiss, you will be missed.

You can walk off, but I can't be your staircase.

One thing I remember when I was just a child,

You used to tell me how you see love in my eyes.

We were only kids, playing along the rides,

Watching all the people spilling all the lies.

One thing I remember when I was just a child,

We used to build high walls afraid to let it fall.

Holding it like a castle; waiting for the war,

One that came and went on, so the wall came down.

Holding weary flowers till we die,

Holding tiny tear drops till they fall.

We used to cry a lot then, but now it seems,

At last, goodbyes are the best,

Goodbyes are the best,

Goodbyes are the best.

We could have never dreamed,

How far we would come,

Purpose undefined on this journey to the Sun.

Miles away from home; we are so alone,

Little by little growing old,
leaving all the pieces of our
broken souls,
Forgetting everything but our lonely world.
In our lonely world,
Our lonely world.

Holding weary flower till we die,
Holding tiny tear drops till they fall.
We used to cry a lot then, but now it seems,
At last, goodbyes are the best,
Goodbyes are so sad.
There's nothing I remember of the time
that has passed,
In the end, my life it's only sand and ash.
Crying for our losses but smiling for the cause,
I see through my windshield,
The world is on the run.

All we have now is all we need,
All we have now is all we need,

All we have now is all we need,
All we have now is all we need.
My heart is pounding out of beats,
Making love on these cold sheets,
Reading the same old tweets,
Can't seem to speak how I feel.

Wish you were here with me,
Through the night to our dreams,
Waking up to the Sun's beams,

Caged forever in the fast lanes,
On an endless road, I'm miles away.
Coming and going, lost and dazed,
I'm here without you again,
Feeling blue in the cold rain,
Just the memories remain.
I see you, getting mesmerized.

The watcher came inside,

Stared into my eyes, and stayed for the night.

We lit up a candle and started a firefight.

She whispered in my ear,

"Darling, I'm here with you tonight,

Just hold me tight,

Through dark and light,

And never say,

Never say goodbye,

To make love out of nothing,

There's no coming back from the other side.

There are no words to describe,

When you are waiting for the last train to pass by.

Eyes that light up the dark sky,

With millions of new horizons to pass by.

They glanced at each other with a smile,

They crossed their paths on a lost mile.

It was nothing less than a bliss,

Take him in and give him a kiss.

Every time you were near; he couldn't resist,

For the love, he couldn't persist.

He gave in to the emptiness inside,

To the deep and dark abyss.

He gave in to the love he missed,

Missing those nights that just perish.

Leaving behind memories we cherish,

Always a feeling left unsaid.

Always these words misread,

My love for you is turning into shreds.

I sail the wind when you come into my mind,

Now I can't feel you, I'm numb inside.

I'm coming back; back again to my senses,

I'm falling out of love,

And flying to the stars.

I'm coming out of love

And flying to the stars

Left you in a burning car,

Your lipstick left a scar,

A burning rose with a thorn so sharp,

So I closed my eyes to curb the pain,

Slipped into a dream,

And fell out of love.

I woke up to see,

You were never mine,

It was all just in my mind.

Some are waiting for the rain

Some are out racing trains

Binding the watch with chains

Some hate what they've become

Some are just lost; never to return

And this is what's come to be

I'm walking to the end

And the end is waiting for me

I sit by my window

And watch the colours change

Waiting for the shadows

To come and take me again

I hold my gaze

And watch the rain

Scattering around like the stars

I sit alone and count the days

Remembering your face

Your red dress and your cherry lips

Your black eyes and your dreary scripts

I still think about you to this day

My heart is full of things to say

Would you listen, or push me away

My lost city girl

Dreaming of a better world

Dreams come like waves

And waves crash into your face

And you stand alone, wretched and defaced

With scattered pieces all around the place

Will the castles of hope rise again,

Will the buried faces rise again.

Even if from my sight you are gone, you arise

With that frown and a smile

I could smell you from a mile

You get one chance with no trial

Alchemy starts in a while

Ran into the devil with red eyes

He greeted me in a style

Said there's no difference between you and I

It's just a waste of the time

Pull their veil off

Look into their eyes

What you'll see is me in a disguise

Now look at it from the devil's eye

He said I'll grant you a life; only if you'll let me take it, when it's time.

I said, 'I've been running for a while

And now I'm tired of these miles

Take what you want, but you can't live my life

One last time I'll try

To hold on to these slipping boots

After that, I promise to let go lose

Let go of this merchandise

Turn around and tread around

Racing to the afterlife

Some estranged nails that held you tight

It feels like the last breath of my life

As these waves held me high

I learned to touch the sky

Went through the changes

I saw my life flashing like the moonlight

In a box of surprise

In a book of rhymes

With turning pages that never compile.

A life that can't be lived, if you can't die

Sometimes I hide oceans in my eyes

Sometimes I fly all alone in the sky

Sometimes I sleep with open eyes

Sometimes I dream from deep inside

There is a jigsaw that is broken apart

It's like my heart but my heart has a missing part

Remind me to love, your love, our love,

old-fashioned love, no matter what.

It's hard for me to keep a check on time

When you say it's all a lie

I search for the fire like a moth ready

to die for its light

Yeah, sometimes I hide from

the Sun cause' it's too bright

Sometimes I run to the rain,

just to drain down the lane

Sometimes I climb the stairs,

never to come back again

Sometimes I learn from their mistakes,

Just to do it again

When it comes to the end,

Tears are my only friend.

When it shines and a shadow comes

crawling upon your mind,

A wavering smile out of the disguise,

To hide the truth that lies behind.

When the ship you've been waiting

for sails away into the Sun,

Leaving you behind and marooned

with a suitcase and a gun.

Tracks lead you to the last train a

nd you die on a run,

Where life moves so fast and death greets

so slow and takes you

along for so long,

My love, so long into the dark hole

Leaving home toward inception,

Fading trails of past perception.

Another fork with no connection,

Chasing dreams to find perfection.
All in search of name, fame, and glory,
In your mind an unfurling wherry.
Drifts away in a sound memory, so heavenly,
A mystery revolving, you get it,
and the end of the story.

Looking up to your heroes, as they fly high,
In a place where even the stars die.
Under the Sun we all rise,
In a place, where no one gets out alive.
Where life glows as the light and death
dims like the night,
Where life moves so fast and death greets
so slow and takes you along for so long,
My love, so long into the dark hole.

Last night was a ball, a big party hall filled

with boys and girls. There was a note in the dresser,

from some woman named Charlotte. Who finally

had found a reason to be free and talked about

her affair in Greece.

No one lends a helping hand,

So I'm holding hands with uncertainty,

And reaching for a foreign land.

I'm burning bridges that can no longer stand,

Moving past a storm, stuck in the sand.

Maybe I'm bound to fall back down,

When nothing waits for me in the clouds.

Don't want to circle around, round and round.

Point me to a place where I can feel safe and sound.

Come closer and grasp what you can't hold,

Go deeper and find what you were never told.

You think it's over and done when it's just begun,

Ride the tide to the moon, dust it off, and run.

Done and dumb, it's time to come

Keys to the door are lost in your soul,

Take the blame and make the change.

Every scar has a story,

So turn the page to the last page.

Some days I feel like I'm not alone,

My shadow haunts me like a ghost.

Some days when I'm on the road,

Some turns take me all around the world.

Some days when I'm on my own,

I lose the sense of this blue world,

With eyes lost between the known

and the unknown, you reach for

the stars but fall by the weight of the world.

You come all alone and you leave on your own,

You crawl and you stroll, and

you prowl and you fall, and

you laugh and you cry and

you try to love and fly.

You do what you can do and then you realize.

You spend your days in a benighted place,

You lose your mind in finding your place,

you try to burn into your own flames.

Cold rain and summer breezing,

White snow and colours springing.

These feelings kept me changing,

Till the day it got me believing.

I can’t turn this page by myself,

These words could never portray self,

How much a man can take is way above me.

And the silence in the breeze was

blowing like a scream.

As I set my sail into the forbidden sea,

Following the reflection of the moon,

In search of a new horizon, a new place to croon.

When I sailed into the forbidden sea,

Onto the strangling waves,

Reaching higher and higher,

Pulling me deeper and deeper.

So come and take my hand,

Help me withstand

These strangling waves,

Reaching higher and higher,

Pulling me deeper and deeper

Would you help me stand,

On this forbidden sea,

I'm sailing away, I'm going all the way,

Follow me into the forbidden sea,

I'm out of here, far away in the forbidden sea.

I don't know what to do,

I've got no clue.

I handed out all my thoughts to you,

And you brushed me off like dust.

Now that I disapprove,

Lost in a place where nothing is found,

Lost in a girl that never comes around,

Lost in a sound that never resounds.

Searched for the road to your heart,

But I took a wrong turn and got lost,

Now I'm looking for another start,

Part torn apart and now I got to part with you.

But I have to jump-start my heart, and it's not for you.

In the end, I have to burn,

To be the light in the dark tunnel.

All these years are just a mere history,

Where love is just a memory.

I've been walking these streets all alone,

Just trying to catch the last train,

To take me away; far away to the

tall east mountains

Where the stars don't shine the same.

The desperate scream of clouds

bursts down into rain,

Falling endlessly through the cold years.

You learn to steer your pain,

You lock the door and forget about the day,

When your heart knows more;

More than they will ever know.

Since that winter, this heart is frozen,

This is not what I have chosen.

You learned so well how to break hearts,

So you won't be the one broken apart.

In a place where love is a shot in the dark,

A lost word to bind back the souls apart,

A forgotten thing for us, and to be who we are.

So I’m walking down the empty streets,

Looking for an empty seat on the last train.

Come to me like a muse,

Bring me joy in my blues.

Spread your wings and learn to fly,

Look up and transcend to the sky.

There's no time to apologize,

Now that I have realized.

Find me a map to the new star,

I'm drifting away in my car.

I heard a word from afar,

We are who we are

I think it's not very far,

Now that I have realized.

I'm reaching out to the new star.

Change me with your touch,

Feel the rush of my blood.

Curtains of clouds fall with a thundering thud.

Tell us all again,

How it all began.

Make them all believe,

Why we are here again

Death calls out your name,

Hide your face in shame.

Tell them you know a way,

But you are lost just the same.

Let the sun today,

Keep shining all the way.

Let the rain today,

Keep falling all in vain.

Send them all away,

Back from where they came.

Fill your mouth with words,

That speaks all your disdain.

As the dust rises,

When the sky crashes,

All logics and reasons fail.

Ruins of yesterday linger and stain

Come down from your high ground,

And watch it all go up in flames.

Something is not in its place,

There's still time to steer away.

There are shadows crawling in my head,

They come alive when I go to bed.

Look into my eyes, they have a story to tell,

Can you hear the dead?

Do you believe what they said,

In the pages of history?

Within the silence, they are led.

She whined about her pain,

As the clouds collapsed into the rain.

Soon after that, the Sun came,

And the barren land sprouted again.

Some things change, some remain,

Others just fall and faint.

I, I could do more than just smile.

I can long to belong somewhere, anywhere but here.

She aimed a dart on my heart,

Bullseye, she tore it apart.

I gave my heart to a girl after a heart attack,

Nothing new, just some love gone bad.

Heartbreaks and heartaches.

Feeding on her fears, a ghost makes it clear

Grab a broom and groom that stare.

If you go to the turn and learn,

To meet your fear,

Feel the chills that spike your skin,

Holding on like icicles.

You try to run but barely move a limb,

One last step from falling,

Now I see you crawling.

Come around, let yourself go to the turn,

And learn to meet your fear,

Before it climbs up your stair,

Drag you down till you lose your stare.

Drag you down and you drop a tear,

Drag you around like a bitch on a leash,

Keep you alive till you lose your sleep

Love your beast

Face your beast

You are the beast.

All alone in the woods,

Clouds glide through the moonlight,

Some are darker and some pass the light.

Let me be, rolling in my strolling truck,

Making my turn, steering till it burns.

I stepped on the accelerator,

And forgot I had brakes,

Raced along the train,

Going off the tracks,

I’m out of this maze.

Washed my windshield with the rain,

Rolled in my tint drape,

Falling into the rally of the apes.

The sun is out again and I’m waiting for the rain.

I'm waiting, and there's no one around.

I'm still waiting for this dream to move on,

And don't you wonder why I'm still holding on?

That you can only dream now, so dream now forever.

I've said so many things

that I couldn't even spell,

But some things can be heard

even if you can't tell.

As the wave falls into the silent night,

You try to run and hide,

But there is nothing that can suffice

What you had in your mind.

I've seen everything there's to see

Thing's that can't be unseen

And found a reflection of me

In everything, there's to be

In a place that can be better

If we just let it be

If we just turn to see

The stone you carry inside yourself

It's too much to take on

Don't you wish sometimes?

This weight to just lift off

So you could just take off

With the wings on your shoulders

To the light, you used to dream of.

When you can't seem to find your heart

Pushed into sharp edges in the dark

Searched everywhere for the missing part

Learned to love with a broken heart

When it all goes in vain and you start again.

What remains are the parts that will

guide you through the cold rain

From the dust, you will rise again.

I'm out in the dark,

Digging my way to another day.

I'm lost and amazed,

I'm digging a grave,

Burying it with my pain.

Everything is drenched in rain,

I was told nothing remains,

No, nothing remains.

It's cold tonight,

Through the trees,

A gale of wind gusts by,

Sending shivers down my spine.

I still hear that wicked voice,

Telling me no lies.

I still see your pretty face,

Crying and frowning in my mind.

I miss her warm skin,

And those wide eyes,

But I am digging a grave,
I'm calling to the waves

Everything is painted grey,
I'll see you on the other side of the page.
I was told nothing remains. Still, something remains

If nothing is meant to stay forever,
why wait till something changes
for better or worse?
Let it all go today,
spend each day like the end is on its way.
Moon bloomed out like a flower,
With petals of light, glowing in the dark.
Another day came and passed by,
She still sings in New York.

Under the shadow of a tree,
She is breathing freely,
Feels like the daylight
Is all that she will need.

Feels like the starlight
Is all that she will see.

Everyone's got a fight to fight,
A battle to win and love to find.
To see through the window,
When the dust settles down,
To see it all as it is known
To know what wasn't shown.

I want to ride with you in a coffin,

If love is dead, we'll scoot for it.

I'm neither your king nor are you queen,

This whole kingdom is obscene,

Why don't we just burn it to ashes

with a matchstick.

These flames look majestic now,

nothing can stop it, but these gathered

masses are acting like plastic.

It's a black summer, these winds will just ignite it,

We don't need it, your majesty, you can have it.

We'll leave it all behind.

We'll sing; till the music, we will find,

We'll dance till the Sun shines.

Hold my hand,

Understand and climb this pyramid of sand.

I am just a newborn,

Born on this sundered land.

Picture two falling hearts,

Never falling apart.

Now that I see you in me and me in you

If the dark calls me too soon,

Will you be waiting for me,

By the sun, like the morning dew?

Hold my heart,

It's steady and ready to be yours in parts.

You were just a newborn,

Born too high in the sky.

Picture two fallen hearts,

Learning to fly.

Now that I see you in me and me in you.

When the time is not on my side,

I hope my prayers would be answered,

So I'll find you by my side.

Who will save us from tomorrow,
It's a walk to the grave.
All you have is, all you gave.
Learn to live and ride the wave.

All caught up in paradise,
Beneath the hell, above the heaven
You will find your answers
In the song unsung; on a walk to the grave.

She comes from the Sun to me,

She falls from the sky for me.

She splatters colours into the breeze.

She is an angel,

She is my sunshine,

Nothing speaks to me as your eyes do.

Look into my eyes and see what they do.

People just break hearts to give it a shape,

Just like a diamond, hard and clean,

So cut it deep and tear it out of me,

Make it beat like you please,

Make it bleed, put it to sleep;

There's too much inside of me

that you just haven't seen,

But there's something inside of me

That isn't for me, so free me from anything

and everything that weighs me down like gravity.

Tear me open, let me breathe,

Break me even, let me see it settle

down like sand flakes in the sea.

Let me go, it's not for me,

I've taken my beating and fallen asleep,

Crying till the last drop of a tear fell out of me.

It's not so easy, no one said it will be,

So let me go, it's not for me.

You can have it all,

I'm leaving it all behind, just like the leaves of the fall

You can either love or you can play the game,

But when it rains, rains, rains,

Everybody loses the game.

You can either love or you can stay sane,

But when it rains, rains, rains,

Everyone loses their brain.

So when it turns grey and the stars disappear,

Lights get blown away,

You hear her call out your name,

And you turn around to see her face,

But all you see is falling rain.

It's been a long cold night, so go away,

Let my sunshine come again,

My only still flame under the falling rain.

I'll look for you in every drop of the rain.

I'll be gone, so long before this storm,

Now would you trust in me, love?

Would you do, would you love me, darling.

What would you do?

When the first sunbeam of the day

fell upon my eyes,

The unwavering sky became brighter

and pulled me higher.

Then as the sun turned black and

left me no other way.

I saw my reflection strip away,

Through the passage of gloom,

There was a room on fire.

“Come inside and warm your soul”,

A friendly voice came to conspire.

They are at war with a self they've made.
They can destroy what they create,
just to enrich their grave.
Unfurling the flag they could never raise,
They came back with a depraved mask
in which they misbehaved.
But this time, they are not hiding their face.

There are things they wish they could change,
Some pieces of them that they could rearrange,
One dream that shapes their nights and days,
And one truth that always remains.
It could just fall from the clouds like rain,
Allowing them to get a view of the clear
blue sky again. So, they take it all in and
wind in search to find it all again
What lies behind those colossal heights
in another place, Sailing down the river
and finding a place to rest their headspace.

Just like the first sun's beam of the day,

With thunder in her eyes, she awakes,

And watches as the whole world

ignites in flames.

She walks down the aisle, stops,

and thinks for a while,

Now what's there to find?

I might just go back and start a new life,

But the things beyond her reach

tugged on a thin line.

So she gave everything to a man

sailing down the river,

With nothing left to confide,

they sailed on as the river took them inside.

For it is said their voices still echo

as the waves collide.

I sit alone at night, watching the moon.

Days passed by, and nothing changed my mood.

After one stormy night,

The moon spoke through the gloom.

I sat alone that night, dancing to its tune,

As the clouds made way for me to reach the moon.

I've tasted the venom of the sweetest fruit,

I've spent nights in a shelter with no roof.

You had the time to watch me suffer,

But no time to call your lover.

You are the ocean and I'm the stream,

falling for you.

I want to steal some light from the sun,

And see it shine in you.

Let these words sink into your mind,

It's hard to stop the sky from falling,

But my arms are wide open tonight.

Let yourself go where the wind blows,

And we'll find our place together.

Let yourself go where the wind blows,

And we'll build this home, however.

We will dance to our heartbeats,

We will sing like the falling beads,

Through the wanton breeze,

Under the wavering trees.

Shadows will grow,

And the fire will rise,

Like the smoke, we will fly,

Like a fool who will try,

Use a tool and pull out your eye.

Dancing with our heartbeats

Singing like the falling beads

Going where our heart beats

I want to steal some dark from the clouds,

And put a drop of rain in your eyes.

Let these words sink into your mind,

It's hard to stop the sky from falling,

But my arms are wide open tonight.

Now I think we're sinking;

We're sinking together this time.

Let yourself go where the wind blows,

And we'll find someplace together.

Let yourself go where the wind blows,

And we'll build this home, however.

We will dance to our heartbeats,

We will sing like the falling beads.

A turn in the alley led to the valley,

Screech from a beak to reach and breach the peak.

Few empty seats and a dirty sheet,

Shelves filled with food to eat and gas to heat.

Selling stones for bones to be

thrown in a cone-shaped home,

Leaving dead skin to scratch

And an old soul to snatch.

When the sun falls,

There's nothing to catch.

I've got skills that can kill,

You say it's a run of the mill.

Now it's time to step up or step aside,

Went inside a tunnel of thoughts and

broke a war inside.

Someone knocked at my door,

And flaming rock fell down on the floor.

I watched the white dove unfurl its wings

into the sky as the Nations collide.

It's not a drill when black ink licks and

leaks on a sheet of bricks, Collapsing every

domino that sticks in front like a deceiving trick.

When it's to die or kill, it's not enough

to just stand still. Take your happy pill and

dwell deep into the rabbit hole.

And if you find the rabbit, you know

You are in the wrong hole.

Nothing left to cry about

Waiting for words to screech out,

Or should I drown here tonight,

In your memory.

That look in your eye,

That once caught my eye,

Is still framed in my heart,

In your memory.

In the darkness of the night,

There's still some light,

That still shines so bright,

In your memory.

But moments just fly by,

Like a raven into the night,

And death takes one last stride,

In cold memory.

The wind turns the pages of the book,

***We once tried to burn*.**

It's easier now to think how much it burns,

Just to let go of the things,

I once held near and dear.

I'll come to terms with her ghost.

In my dream, I fear.

It was good for a while,

But this fleeting time.

Now if there's a heaven,

We will walk it forever.

Through the gates of hell,

To the limitless sky.

Through the burning fields,

Watch the starlet die.

In the virgin sea,

I set myself free.

I killed your memory

I killed your memory

I killed your memory

You used to be so strong,

Before the burst of storm,

Hear the crack of storm,

The rally of the rumbling clouds,

Covering the sky grey in frost.

As the rain knocks on the roof,

Sliding down your windowpane,

As the world weeps in the haze,

Lightning strikes your face,

Obscuring by the space

Come with me into the dark,

To the last turn of the road,

On the next page of the end,

Beyond the world, you can comprehend,

It's waiting to take you away.

To the end of your long run,

The end of a deep burn,

Where the sun never comes,

You're the lamp that lights the night,

And you will be star-high.

In the darkness hides the light,
In your eyes, it resides,
Peel away your face of charade,
Don't hide buried alive,
Bring us closer to the stars,
Take us closer to Mars.
It's taking longer than I thought,
Why it always got to be so far,
So far away in the dark,
So far away from the grasp,
So star-high in the night,

Shine down, starlight.
Take me on another ride,
Take me star-high,

Hold me together before I fall apart,

This roller coaster is going too far,

Gliding on a feather of the night,

Wondering if it would make things right.

No, we can't look back, it's all black,

No, we can't run away, there's no track,

No, we can't give in to these feelings,

That comes to us in the dark,

That takes us to our home,

To the last turn of the long road.

I could keep my heart silent,
And my mind hushed,
With a soft touch of her lips.

I can sing till I can't sing anymore,
And dance till my feet become sore,
With her sound in my soul.

I can lose it all in a beat,
And sit alone and weep,
With her smile curling me in.

I wanted to stay there all night,
Had nothing better on my mind,
With her by my side.

We brought the moon to light,
I had seen it in her eyes
My heart raced but didn't touch the finish line,

The cold wind blew into our faces,

With dust hindering sight,

With crystal-cooled water, we washed our eyes.

It was dark, too dark to see,

To lose ourselves and find the lost paradise.

But the moment was gone and left

behind a stale storm.

With dreams in hand,

we strolled in those reckless times,

Wanton waves came rolling by,

Droll thoughts stocked embers into the sky.

On one of those blue days,

The wind blew and we parted ways.

There's an unheard voice that yearns to sing.

Chained against the walls, dragged along the halls.

Beaten, bruised, and hushed,

Left to rot in the boiling sun.

A voice that croons for the death of love.

A sound so soft, that it can hurt no one.

Music, so immaculate, it plays for everyone.

It's been knocking on your door,

Rolling in your dreams,

Jiving in the breeze, calling your name,

to let it go free.

Wild horse chariots carrying the melody

A rabbit has to dig its hole, rabbit's only home.

He's tired and old, his skin so cold.

But as the deadly claws come close,

Rabbit digs another hole.

In the labyrinth below, it gets swallowed.

A glimmer in the breeze, a free-falling stream,

Dense trees in the shimmering carefree dream.

Bury the burrow and let the wheels roll.

Rabbit dig another hole.

Can't you see wonders waiting at your brink?

Step out, you've always been free,

Run wild and free into the breeze;

Let those wings stroke the wind,

Spatter out the true colours from within.

Don't gulp that voice, let it sing,

Let it wash away all the faded tints.

My mind's opaque, reflecting your bleeding heart,

Bow-tied tourniquet tearing apart.

Soul slithering for stripping procession,

Hands tied for mental perversion.

Love flourished, then quickly vanished,

Carnival lit up with enticing colours.

The gathered crowd started to roll and rumble,

Twisting, turning flock of weathering feathers,

Running to the closest, door of the harlequin.

A dream untouched like a maiden,

A place unmapped, far away from the borders.

Unblemished feeling like bliss in disguise.

Where the serenity lies in an unfettered weeping child.

You exude from the Sun like its sunshine.

Your rapturous gestures would not lie.

Dancing in the backyard even after the clock chimes,

Darkening the sky like a candle burning through the night.

There she was in blue, teasing the flowers with ten thousand hues.

In her garden where I play the blues.

In her arms, I lay confused.

In my mind, she is cooped.

My ear yearns for the nightingale that has flown by.

My weary eyes still search for you; in every nest, and on every tree.

After the sun drowns in the ocean, on the sheen sea,

Even where the moon could be seen.

Running away, why do you always keep running away?

Come and lay beside me; open up your scars to me,

Let me kiss away your pain.

You are everywhere, even in my veins;

Let me recite my poetry to you, without any refrain.

Look at the wavering clouds, learning to fly,

With their watering eyes, look how they fly

Tiny droplets of marionettes, fall like a broken rosary in a plight.

And now that you've fallen apart,

Pull your head out of the clouds.

Stand out of the crowd, and step back on the ground.

Come and take a look all around;

Those fallen pieces can't be found.

Rivers in which you used to dive have also drowned

You can drift away beyond the horizon

Like a capsized rusted boat resting in a dust bowl.

Dabbling in your fish bowl,

Until the dust get blown away

How still the solid ground pulls you under the patterns of the bay

Sprouting out new kinds with vague aplomb,

Look how they waver in the ease of the zephyr,

Look at their critique smile, journey into the wild Nile.

Your boat waits in the charnel house,

Solemnly waiting for you to give you a ride.

My solace is now a colorless spring, my tears just a sweet rill.

Dancing in the dead of the night with no hopes to thrill.

I drained the juice of life, from the pain purging from within.

Getting lost in the remembrance of love,

Smiling and curling in the clouds above,

Embracing this thing called love.

Counting my memories, my lonely ones.

My words gushed out, death of my only one.

I searched and lurked with a pounding heart, in my awakening thoughts,

Ran away as far as I could,

Turned around, and there it was the shattered truth.

Slithering like a shadow it pursued.

Gasping as the fantôme vanished into the thin air,

Leaving behind a putrid perfume.

Laughed like a joker even though the joke was a bore,

Begged like a hooker cause' I had lost my only hope,

So I danced till I parched out with a lone jingle.

We gazed and we gazed then even the stars dissembled.

We stared and we stared till the stars disassembled

I'm estranged from the past, stranded by the coming future.

Dancing in the burning pyre of Juncture, elongating this confusion without conjecture.

Knocking on the doors of perception, a helping hand with no connection

Feeling blue but merging with cosmic hues,

Longing clues in the insights of the cruise.

Strangling gale teasing you, destined time will be over soon.

Dripping sand in the bottomless jar gliding through,

Falling rain in the fathomless clepsydra splashing through.

Filling the gaps with the silent enclosure,

Heeding eyes leading to disclosure.

Feasting gut with innumerable questions,

Wandering ways lead to one conjunction.

My mind aches and my heart breaks,

Trembling feet dabbling in the blood with no ache

Screeching much too loud, reaching up to the cloud,

And falling back on the ground with a thud sound.

Thoughts shattering, silence surrounds,

Voices that are left unheard even by the gods.

Deathly Hallow surrounds in the valley of the lost,

Where there is ordnance, and the flowers crumble in the yearning of the Sun.

The last chord he heard was the sound of a gun.

Their malleable chains try to bind them as they run,

Steering envy in the house of the setting sun.

People are on the run but the spite catches them with a stun.

Skirmish begins with vague awareness, thoughts evoke to kill the feeble one.

For who is the angel and who is the demon, under the sky, they all look one.

Everyone believes they have the right reason, assuring they are the chosen one.

Who plays the fool? Who cries in woe? Who is who? And who are you?

Digging a shallow grave, one that droops.

Drenching himself in an unkind disease, he goes through throes.

Agreement of truce goes untouched, white cloth washed in serpent's blood.

A bird with a broken wing still searching for love; caged in its feathers, they called it a dove.

Another full circle is spiralling down,

Another candle blew in the ghost town.

Venom drips from her like spittle,

Her voice screeches like a hungry falcon.

Her eyes purging for heaven,

Lost in her arms of obsession.

She searches and dreams in confessions,

Holding her grudge inside,

feeding her temptations.

She laments for her expression,

as she got her sanction.

She trusts her inception but

disgusts her reflection.

Her heart is shaped like a luring imprisonment

eggshell.

She confides a facade to feed her nectar.

She lost her smile, in the gloom she gestures.

In different moods, she falls like feathers.

She oozes in thoughts and severs the clots.

She surges the pain,

and in copulation she sustains.

I'm the poet and she is my bane.

I blame myself for falling in her perfidious love, how insane I thought she was the one.

She amputates my heart cause' she has none.

I smiled and asked her, Isn't it fun.

It's easier to blame someone else,

Cause' it's harder to believe you

could do something wrong.

You were all that I ever wanted

but now I wish you to be gone,

And I can finally get a chance to be alone;

it's not that I hate you,

Cause' you don't really matter at all.

I can't love you as you wished

on those lonely nights,

I'm a monster hiding in the closet

of a lonely bride.

I've come to wash that maybelline face

and leave a scar on that pretty smile.

You pull the trigger, and my heart hangs in a flitter

You tie the noose, and my head bangs in jitter.

You try to smother me, but

Your last breath is my resurrection

Your tear drops are my affection

And my laughter is your mysterious affliction.

Accept or have the guts to disrespect.

Bust love and blame it on trust,

must the lust get trapped in cocks and cunts?

Don't wait till the dust turns you into rust.

Time strips and slips, it clicks and ticks,

and it's never fixed, just watch its

sticks and tricks.

When it pricks, you grapple with

the needle to stitch it inch by inch.

But it's getting late,

blood rushes out with hate.

Death knocks at your face and

opens up the gate, tugging you around,

it flips the page like the sky falling

down to retrace.

It summons you for the last dance and

gives you a funny face, strikes out your name.

Burning down the sage,

flowers bloom in her grace.

Can't remember her face,

but still beautiful to embrace.

It's a rap, don't stop! Rewind the tape.

These words are put down in shape, to efface your trace, captivating to transcend your state, capsizing in the horizon to integrate with the sensation of attraction and alleviating the tension, the story doesn't end here, it refrains, bursting your brain, washing silhouettes.

I'm tired, I'm lonely, I'm slowly

falling into pieces.

I'm dying of feelings, I'm losing the

meaning of everything there is.

I'm horny, it's morning, and I'm waking

up at the deep end.

I'm breathing the fire that comes from the liars,

but I'm still believing.

The clock has been ticking, the hours

have been shifting, and now I'm leaving.

So when I'm gone, just know I had to go

cause' I can't wait here anymore.

There's so much more beyond that door,

That I am missing, and I don't want to

miss a thing anymore.

Sing to me your freedom song

In a place where it's long gone

Let me ring the frantic bell

Breaking down the hell's bell

Sing to me your love song

In a place where it's long gone

Let me hear my love call, my one and all

Flying away in sweet zephyr

From a place engulfed in hate

From a criticized state

To my one and all

To my one and all

When you come around,

Time catches the speed of light.

Just then, these needles strike rust,

and batteries die.

It's nothing less than a blight,

As time drops from the height.

When you leave my side along the

crashing tides,

I'll colour this canvas red; then I'll kill

you on your bed.

Forget what I said, I'll drown you instead.

What's the use of it anyway,

When you are not here?

Why would you even care?

Waiting for this moment to appear

Come and now break this pair

End it now and disappear.

When I'm gone away,

Would it break your heart

To see me walk away?

Would you come along

To solace where your heart belongs?

Even when I'm far away,

You are my hideaway.

Even when I close my eyes,

We keep making my fire rise.

I'm in solace where our heart belongs,

I've got you framed in my thoughts,

The sun and the moon also seem to know

That love doesn't hurt anyone.

It's the absence of it that keeps eating you.

Desolate hours with deserted feelings,

You know this love can't be fixed.

There is so much more for the seeking.

But I don't want to fall behind,

There is so much more to find.

I need something more to breathe,

So come and give yourself to me.

Keep running the circle, mice, you will get your cheese slice, throw away the dice.

Keep rolling to the sunrise, come to the other side,

Come on to me, come to the end, come step on the ride.

Sleep on me tonight

When you close your eyes in the dim night,

I turn off the light and roll by your side,

Holding you tight like a broken glass,

Scared to pull you out of my mind.

I'm setting my stakes up high,

Marking these stairs with a legacy to leave behind.

We two are not alike,

You like to play with this heart of mine.

I like to lay your heart on mine,

You're falling hard like every time.

Eyes don't lie, you don’t even realize

Can't help but wish you'd never leave,

I'm spinning my wheels, how once I used to dream.

What good will come from counting and breaking the same old beads

Horns of a crown are growing thorns out of the thrones of stone,

Groaning for the hope that has faded to the unknown.

I'm riding towards the plight; darkness is confining me, I'm losing my sight,

Heard you moved on,I lost my fight,

Getting along the shadow of the night.

I'm dying of love with no one to call mine,

You took off blowing smoke on my face but it's fine

There's a man on the barren road,

Drifting under a load of the sky,

With an empty stomach and gritting teeth, with stories untold, and a lethal mind.

A man walks, dressed up like a clown,

To wash his face in the dusty dry storm.

Waiting for the sun, but rain comes down.

I'll wait here, I'll do you no harm.

Forget about the mind, in breathing out I feel alive.

A new tree will grow if we shed some new light,

Dropping my mic, that's a joke, my friend.

Gravity doesn't lie.

As you rolled your eyes back,

I sat there all night,

Holding a candle in the snuffed-out moon.

When all the flames slithered down,

I stripped back into my room.

Holding on to you like screws in a coffin,

And my pen like a blade

To fade away into a shade

To cut through this page

To spell down my rage

It sounds like; great!

It's full of rage, lend me your ear and engage,

Break free from your cage.

Don't lend me your pity and cross your heart for it,

When it's just a pretty old little ditty.

Now don't get sceptical, this isn't very practical,

This was just a jest, of one gest in a gist,

But never a behest.

I want to get locked away with you in a coffin,

And rush into your body like endorphins,

Just want to jump through these waves like dolphins.

Hold my hand and help me stand

You don't know me yet that I can’t stand

I'm not stunned; I'm stung, and strung out and

Succumbed by the bad taste of your tongue.

So let me run, and race with a bullet coming out of a gun

With eyes as red as the setting sun,

Is there a thing called a naked nun?

I want to get things done.

The image might look odious,

And sound a little too hideous,

But blame the world for sticking a penis in the anus,

No disrespect to the famous methodical son to detain us.

Anyone can learn to catch the yellow bus, thus you are ignoramus,

Look carefully, it's not a cross, what is it then?

Let it be x

The End

www.ingramcontent.com/pod-product-compliance
Lightning Source LLC
LaVergne TN
LVHW091328150826
845673LV00006B/1802

* 9 7 9 8 8 9 0 6 7 4 8 8 3 *